FRIENDS
OF ACPL

RELIGIONS OF HUMANITY

LC 6/4/08

Chelsea House Publishers
1974 Sproul Road, Suite 400
Broomall, PA 19008

The Chelsea House
world wide web address is
www.chelseahouse.com

First Printing

1 3 5 7 9 6 4 2

Library of Congress
Cataloging-in-Publication
Data Applied For:
ISBN: 0-7910-6629-0

Design
Jaca Book

Original English text by
Lawrence E. Sullivan

*A Protestant church stands among the skyscrapers of Manhattan.*

*Opposite: The public hall that serves as a room for meetings, debates and conferences, as well as a house of worship in the ecumenical Agape Center, near Prali (Turin, Italy), managed by the Waldensian community, which has been a part of the Protestant Reformation since 1532.*

# LAWRENCE E. SULLIVAN

## THE THESES OF
# PROTESTANTISM

CHELSEA HOUSE PUBLISHERS
PHILADELPHIA

*The imposing 19th century wood-carved pulpit in the Waldensian church at Pramollo (Turin, Italy), in front of which is placed an open Bible.*

# CONTENTS

# INTRODUCTION

"Place God first, above all things." This is the prophetic message of all Protestant reformers. On the one hand, the message was a rebuke, a *protest* in the manner of Old Testament prophets, against practices and beliefs of the Roman Catholic Church that, in the view of reformers, obscured God's supreme power by posing as perfect and taking the place of God's authority. When church authorities present themselves as infallible or when sacramental actions, dogmatic beliefs, governing institutions, holy art objects, or philosophical certitudes appear ultimate or absolute, this idolatry should be criticized as such and rejected. On the other hand, the Protestant message exhorted the believer to stand and give credible witness (*pro-testari*, to testify) to the truth of God's saving grace. Different reformers made these points in distinct ways with long-lasting effects. Indeed, many Protestants are proud of the plural expressions that have blossomed as a result of the Protestant Reformation. In the chapters that follow, the abiding insights and expressions that characterize Protestant belief and behavior are singled out for special attention.

*A ceremony in St. John the Divine Episcopal Cathedral in New York.*

# 1
# PEOPLE OF THE WORD: BIBLE, PREACHING, AND SONG

Protestants are people of the Word, as is evident in their regular common worship. On the Lord's Day, Protestants gather together to hear the Word of God read before the congregation. Being the record of God's Word made known in history, Sacred Scripture is the unrivaled source of revelation and authority, outweighing dogma, magisterial tradition, or the teaching of Pope or bishops. Bible reading is the focal point of Protestant worship, where selections are recited aloud.

In response to God's Word, worshippers usually offer words of their own—words of preaching, prayer, and praise. A minister or other leaders rise to preach a sermon based on

the scripture lesson of the day or give testimony to the Word of God at work within them. The goals of the preached word and testimony is to enlighten the mind, warm the heart, and move the will of the listeners so that they might hear God's Word and keep it. Such goals are arrived at only through the grace of faith, freely given by God. To that end, the preacher may call upon God's Holy Spirit, who inspired the Biblical text in the first place, to grace the listeners with the gift of faith in God's Word.

The congregation responds to God's presence in the Biblical Word with prayers and hymns. These vocal expressions

*1. A glimpse of a sermon: the words of the preacher draw on the Bible that he holds as he addresses the faithful. Augsburg, etching 1530.*
*2. Choir of St. John the Divine Episcopal Cathedral in New York on the occasion of a joint celebration with a group of Native Americans.*

offer praise, petition, and thanks. Words are recited in unison, expressing the conviction that a worshipping congregation is a fellowship of those who have like minds, united with the mind and body of Christ in a communion of saints.

Song plays a special role in Protestant prayer. Important Protestant leaders, such as Martin Luther, John Wesley and Charles Wesley, composed hymns that still mark the worship in the denominations they founded. The diversity of Protestant expressions is evident in the range of Protestant music: from Johann Sebastian Bach to Gospel choirs, Christian rock, and exuberant Pentecostal forms found among the various ethnic and indigenous peoples of the world today. The first book published by Puritan settlers in New England was a Psalter for singing the psalms in worship.

In Jesus Christ the one God revealed himself. Beyond the regular reading of the Gospels, most Protestants commemorate the words and deeds of Jesus Christ at suitable points in the life-cycle of an individual or in the yearly calendar of the community: in Baptism and in the Eucharist.

The architecture of Protestant churches reflects the priority of the Word: giving prominence to the lectern for Scripture reading, the pulpit for preaching, the choir and congregational benches for song and prayer and, where appropriate, also the font for baptism and table for Eucharist.

*3. This illustration from the portrait of gospel singer Bessie Griffin, shows the intensity of the interpretation of the African American spiritual that often had its first performance in church choirs. When asked where she learned to sing Griffin responded without hesitation: "In church, of course!"*

3

# THE CHANGING FACE OF PROTESTANTISM

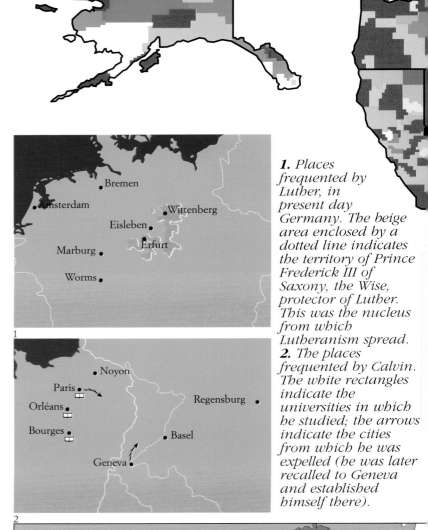

The Protestant movement in Christianity generally refers to reform activities that began in 16th century Europe. Unlike other Christian reform movements that sprang from the monasteries, religious orders, and leading bishops, many Protestant reformers came from universities or academies. Great emphasis was placed on published writings and on the ability of the average worshipper to read those writings. Early Protestant writings are often linked to the widespread use of local languages and the standardization of national languages. Since then, differences in thought, practice, and social or national background have created some 20,000 religious denominations, many of which are linked together in national or international councils or federations. Today, the greatest growth in numbers (if not in wealth and power) has been experienced not in the more highly-educated Northern Europeans and North Americans, but instead in the less wealthy populations of Africa, Latin America, and parts of Asia (including China). Missionaries carried the Protestant message during the 19th and early 20th centuries, where they often functioned with support from colonial governments. However, the most significant transformation of Protestantism since 1900 has taken place in the spread of vibrant forms of Pentecostalism, without state supports and other charismatic movements. Following the experiences of the early Christians described in the first two chapters of Acts, Pentecostalism focuses on the dramatic religious experiences of conversion, sanctification, baptism in the spirit, revival, speaking in tongues, and healing. Launched from such places as Bethel Bible College in Topeka, Kansas, where Charles Fox Parham preached in 1901, and the Azusa Street Apostolic Faith Mission in Los Angeles, founded by Parham's African-American disciple, William Joseph Seymour, in 1906, the Pentecostal movement has spread throughout the world. The charismatic influence has even been felt in the so-called "mainline" Protestant churches. Since the 1950s and the gradual return of former colonies to their native leadership, Pentecostalism has been taken up by native groups, who have added their own particular influences. Of Mexico's seven million Pentecostals, for example, one third are Otomí Indians, while many of the more than 15 million Pentecostals in Africa belong to rapidly growing assemblies founded by native leaders.

*1. Places frequented by Luther, in present day Germany. The beige area enclosed by a dotted line indicates the territory of Prince Frederick III of Saxony, the Wise, protector of Luther. This was the nucleus from which Lutheranism spread.*
*2. The places frequented by Calvin. The white rectangles indicate the universities in which he studied; the arrows indicate the cities from which he was expelled (he was later recalled to Geneva and established himself there).*

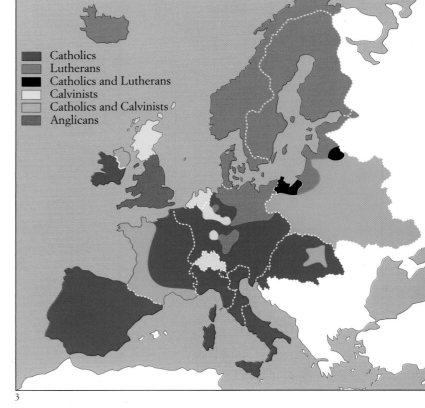

- Catholics
- Lutherans
- Catholics and Lutherans
- Calvinists
- Catholics and Calvinists
- Anglicans

*3. Christian affiliations in Europe at the end of the 16th century.*
*4. The major Protestant denominations in the USA in 1990 (source: "Churches and Church Membership in the United States: 1990," Glenmary Research Center, Atlanta, Georgia, 1992). The corresponding legend is to the right.*
*5. Protestants in the world today. The corresponding legend is to the left.*

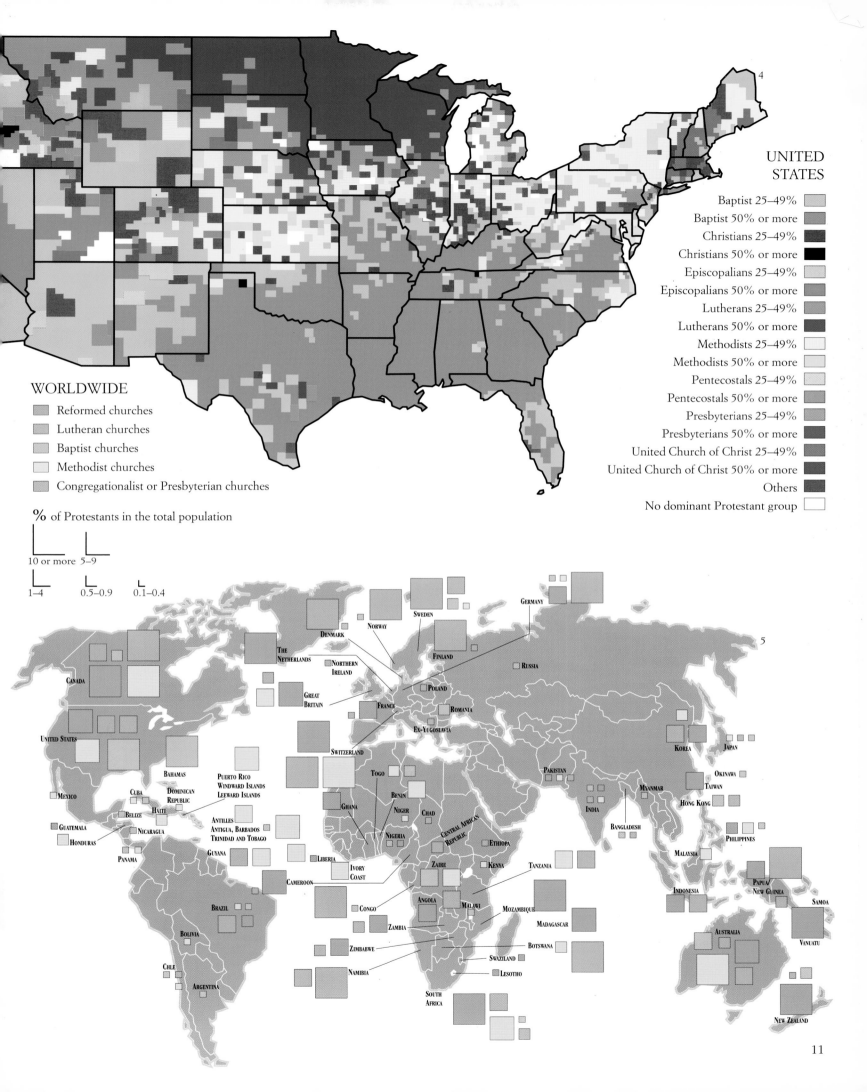

# WORLDWIDE

- Reformed churches
- Lutheran churches
- Baptist churches
- Methodist churches
- Congregationalist or Presbyterian churches

**%** of Protestants in the total population

10 or more    5–9

1–4    0.5–0.9    0.1–0.4

# UNITED STATES

- Baptist 25–49%
- Baptist 50% or more
- Christians 25–49%
- Christians 50% or more
- Episcopalians 25–49%
- Episcopalians 50% or more
- Lutherans 25–49%
- Lutherans 50% or more
- Methodists 25–49%
- Methodists 50% or more
- Pentecostals 25–49%
- Pentecostals 50% or more
- Presbyterians 25–49%
- Presbyterians 50% or more
- United Church of Christ 25–49%
- United Church of Christ 50% or more
- Others
- No dominant Protestant group

CANADA

UNITED STATES

MEXICO

GUATEMALA

HONDURAS

NICARAGUA

PANAMA

BELIZE

CUBA

DOMINICAN REPUBLIC

HAITI

BAHAMAS

PUERTO RICO
WINDWARD ISLANDS
LEEWARD ISLANDS

ANTILLES
ANTIGUA, BARBADOS
TRINIDAD AND TOBAGO

GUYANA

BRAZIL

BOLIVIA

CHILE

ARGENTINA

THE NETHERLANDS

DENMARK

NORWAY

SWEDEN

FINLAND

NORTHERN IRELAND

GREAT BRITAIN

FRANCE

SWITZERLAND

GERMANY

POLAND

ROMANIA

EX-YUGOSLAVIA

RUSSIA

PAKISTAN

INDIA

BANGLADESH

TOGO

BENIN

NIGER

CHAD

GHANA

NIGERIA

CENTRAL AFRICAN REPUBLIC

LIBERIA

IVORY COAST

CAMEROON

CONGO

ZAIRE

ANGOLA

ZAMBIA

ZIMBABWE

NAMIBIA

MALAWI

MOZAMBIQUE

MADAGASCAR

BOTSWANA

SWAZILAND

LESOTHO

SOUTH AFRICA

ETHIOPA

KENYA

TANZANIA

KOREA

JAPAN

OKINAWA

TAIWAN

HONG KONG

MYANMAR

PHILIPPINES

MALAYSIA

INDONESIA

PAPUA/NEW GUINEA

SAMOA

VANUATU

AUSTRALIA

NEW ZEALAND

11

# 3
# "NO OTHER GODS BEFORE ME": LUTHER AND ZWINGLI AS LEADERS OF REFORM

MARTIN LUTHER (1483-1546) pioneered German Protestantism. Born in Eisleben, Germany, and raised in nearby Mansfeld, he entered the Monastery of the Hermits of Saint Augustine at the age of 22, keeping a vow he had made to Saint Anne during a violent storm. He had already completed a master's degree at the University of Erfurt and had begun to study law. But he left legal studies to take up theology, receiving a degree in Biblical study in 1509 from the University of Wittenberg, where he would later teach. Before completing his studies at the University of Wittenberg, he was sent to Rome by the monastery. In Rome, he was dismayed at how worldly the church had become. In his early years of teaching Scripture at the university (1515-1519), he had focused on the issues of sinfulness and saving grace. From his studies and his spiritual experiences, he came to understand a concept of God's righteousness, described by Paul in Romans 1:17, that did not agree with Roman Catholic practices, in particular the idea of indulgences granted by the Church. Luther could not agree that salvation involved a kind of cooperation between God's grace and human work—he believed that salvation came only through God's grace alone, forgiving the sinful human being through a theology of the cross. On October 31, 1517, Luther published his ideas in a work titled *Ninety-five Theses*. In June 1520, the Pope issued his response, condemning as wrong Luther's views in a statement known as *Exsurge Domine* (Arise, O Lord). Luther then took the radical step of burning this papal document in public on December 10, 1520. By 1521, the German legislature had declared him an outlaw. But Luther was not finished with stirring up controversy. In 1525, the same year in which he married, he began to publicize his differences not with Roman Catholic authorities, but instead with other reformers. These disagreements continued and resulted in sharp divisions among Protestants at Marburg in 1529 and Augsburg in 1530, where the first Protestant Confession of Faith was produced. Because of his outlaw status, Luther himself could not be there, but his opinions were presented by other spokesmen, such as Philipp Melanchthon. From 1533-1536, Luther helped with the reorganization of the University of Wittenberg. Until his final days, Luther argued that only the Bible could provide an authoritative picture of God's goodness and grace.

HULDRYCH ZWINGLI (1484-1531) was born in Wildhaus, Switzerland, and studied in Vienna and Basel. He served as a pastor in Glarus and Einsiedeln before becoming a preacher at the Zurich Cathedral in 1518. He remained there for the rest of his life. Like Luther, he spoke out against in-dulgences and stated that the Bible was the ultimate guide for the Christian and the Church. Zwingli believed that Christ's life and death provided the gift of grace—a gift that would take away all sin. For this reason, he rejected the Roman Catholic practices of penances and the idea of Purgatory. He argued his views in his *Sixty-seven Conclusions*, presented at the council of Zurich in 1523, a meeting at which the

*1. A portrait of Martin Luther from the studio of German painter and engraver Lucas Cranach the Elder in 1529, Uffizi Gallery, Florence (Italy).*

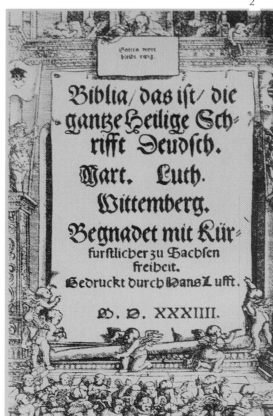

*2. Frontispiece from the German translation of the Bible by Martin Luther, Wittenberg (Germany), 1534.*

*3. Set in Zurich during the era of Huldrych Zwingli, this drawing shows a scene of public discussion, known as "Zurich debate," 1523, in which Zwingli leads the discussion to defend his vision of church reform.*

council ultimately sided with the Reformation. However, Zwingli and Luther did not agree on all points. Zwingli believed that the Lord's Supper, or Communion, did not physically transform the bread and wine into Christ's body, but instead changed the people participating in the Supper, transforming them into saints called by Christ to become members of His church. For Zwingli, this choosing and gathering of the saints by Christ is the true meaning of a church (which has heavenly, historical, and local manifestations), with Christ as a kind of invisible force making possible the visible, gathered church. In Zwingli's opinion, unlike the views of Luther or Calvin, Christ also serves as an authority over the government, which derives its power to gov-

ern from the will of the people whom Christ gathers as a church. Zwingli believed that government is founded on principles of justice revealed in the Bible, and that through preaching, rulers should be taught these principles of Biblical justice. In turn, the government rules over the church and is ultimately responsible for maintaining justice and order. Zwingli supported the suppression of the Catholicism in his part of Switzerland, and also supported the movement, in 1526, to put down the Anabaptists, who disagreed with infant baptism and felt that local congregations, rather than larger churches or civil councils, should have the final say in decisions. Zwingli was killed in a battle fighting the Pope's military forces.

# "DECLARE THE GOOD NEWS": THE MISSION AND METHOD OF CALVIN AND WESLEY

JOHN CALVIN (1509-1564) was born in Picardy, France, where his father served as an attorney to the bishop of Noyon. Calvin earned a Master's degree in theology at the University of Paris, studying there for 11 years before his father, after strong disagreements with the bishop, ordered his son to study law in Orléans. Calvin completed his law degree in three years and, after the death of his excommunicated father, returned to Paris to study. In 1533, he was forced to leave the city when theologians at the university rejected the Lutheran ideas he had woven into a speech given by Nicholas Cop, the university's rector. In July 1536, he moved to Geneva, Switzerland, where he became the brilliant designer of a program of thought and action which included theology, social philosophy, training of ministers and universal mission. He restructured the school system and established the University of Geneva. His preaching was so powerful that it resulted in Geneva's adopting a stricter moral code based on Biblical principles. Calvin possessed a keen intellect, grounded in the humanists' tendency to prize primary sources—in his case the Bible—and favored practical applications of learning. In Calvin's view, the Biblical message was a spiritual one, for the Scripture was inspired by the Holy Spirit and could only be interpreted through the work of the Holy Spirit. The goal of theology, in his view, was not to inspire abstract reasoning, but rather to form a more pious, or spiritual, mind. In 1536, Calvin published a spiritual guide called *Institutes of the Christian Religion*, which emphasized that God created humans to be united with Him through knowledge of God as the Creator and Redeemer. Calvin's idea was that the pious mind, formed by faith, would contain two kinds of knowledge: the knowledge of an invisible God, the hidden Creator of all things from nothing; and the knowledge of a visible God revealed in the history of redemption recorded in the Bible. At the center of these two kinds of knowledge is Christ, the sole mediator through whom God calls sinful individuals and then restores them to the life God intended for them. The Holy Spirit unites humans with Christ, inspiring in them this faith-knowledge that restores union with God. Not wanting to place power in the hands of hierarchical clergy, Calvin designed an organization that gave power to the local church, whose members elect their leaders. Local churches then sent representatives to larger organizations and general assemblies. Calvin believed that churches should be free from governmental control. The Reformed and Presbyterian churches came from this movement and contain the influence of Calvin's thoughts and practices.

JOHN WESLEY (1703-1791) studied at Christ Church, Oxford, and became a fellow of Lincoln College at Oxford after his ordination in the Church of England in 1725. While tutoring at Oxford in 1729, he directed religious study groups, beginning with one formed by his younger brother, Charles. The goal was to revive the spiritual life in these members of the Church of England (which King Henry VIII had separated from Ro-

*1. This drawing portrays the French reformer Calvin in the city of Basel where he wrote his major work "Institutes of the Christian Religion."*

1

man Catholicism two centuries earlier). Through methodical study and reading the classic works of spiritual literature, Wesley and his students rededicated themselves to a Christian life modeled on the early church. The members of these study groups became known as "Methodists." For two years, John Wesley, with the assistance of his brother, Charles, and other Methodists from Oxford, carried out a ministry in Georgia, then an American colony. While Wesley felt that this mission was ultimately unsuccessful, he was impressed by the Moravians he met along the way. Under the guidance of Moravian Peter Böhler, Wesley had a dramatic spiritual awakening on May 24, 1738, during which he experienced Christ as his personal savior from sin and death. He changed his Methodist groups to more closely resemble Moravian organizations, forming small bands of six members, consisting solely of men or women but never both, who shared spiritual experiences. He and his brother published emotional hymns and poems designed to testify to the warming of their hearts and draw other seekers toward the experience of

Christ as their personal Lord and Savior. Wesley believed that, with the saving and perfecting grace of faith, Methodists could triumph over sin and show, through their own good deeds, the goodness of the Holy Spirit. Wesley published his Sermons and outlined the purpose and manner of Methodist preaching in *Explanatory Notes upon the New Testament* (1755). He organized traveling preachers and commissioned laypeople, ordinary believers, to preach as well. His disregard for specific regional parishes, his use of lay preachers, and his organization of groups outside the control of church authorities all created tension with the religious leaders of the Church of England. In 1744, Wesley held the first of an ongoing series of annual conferences that became, many years later, the governing body of Methodism, a new denomination formally established after Wesley's death.

2

3

**2.** *One of the most famous engravings (1751-1752) by William Hogarth, English painter and engraver. Portraying the underworld of London, conceived as a teaching tool, it seeks to illustrate the human misery triggered by alcohol abuse; and it dramatically emphasizes the suffering addressed by the preaching and missionary work of John Wesley of the same period.*
**3.** *John Wesley preaching. Graphic elaboration from a painting by N. Hone, 1766.*

# JUSTIFIED BY FAITH

The apostle Paul wrote in his letters to the Romans and Galatians that "the just shall live by faith." This is an important phrase for Protestant thought, beginning with Martin Luther. In the Protestant view, faith is not simply agreeing with facts for which there is little evidence. Instead, faith involves a complete reorientation of personality, a total transformation in response to God. There is, of course, an intellectual aspect to faith—the knowledge, for example, that God is the infinite and omnipotent Creator who has revealed himself in the history of redemption. But, in truth, this knowledge is really beyond human understanding. Nothing within the sinful, finite self can render it conscious of God's infinite nature and mystery. Moreover, faith is never simply an intellectual understanding, it is also a stirring of the affections, resulting in acts of profound love and trust. And faith is also a revamping of the will, surrendering it to God and becoming thereby God's instrument of love in the world. Nothing within the unaided human self can propel it into the transformed condition of knowledge, affection, and will for which the human was created in the first place.

The energy and understanding that move humans toward this redemptive union with God come from the grace of faith alone. Through the grace of God in faith, humans are made right (*justum facere*), or justified. In this way, the Holy Spirit

*__1.__ Saint Paul seen in a painting on wood from the paleo-Christian era.*
*__2.__ In a Protestant church in New York one of the faithful concentrates amid the crowd.*
*__3.__ "Jesus Saves" is the title of the photograph by Wim Wenders (Houston, TX, USA). The Protestant place of worship highlights the saving action of Jesus.*

draws together the faithful Christian with the saving actions of Jesus Christ, and so restores a right relationship with God the creator as well as a right relationship with all other creatures in the world.

This faith is deeply personal, with its experiential knowledge that God is my God. This is why Protestant reformers rejected the idea that faith, or ultimate justification, came from the routine practice of religious activities. A complete change of heart, through a direct experience of God's saving love, is the key.

For Protestants, sacred Scripture alone offers the authoritative experience of God's creative and saving love. The grace of faith is linked to reading the Bible, since the Bible and the saving events recorded in it are inspired by God's Spirit. The Spirit that hovered over the formless void at the time of creation, the Spirit that came down as tongues of fire on the first believers 50 days after Jesus' obedient death, is the same Spirit who speaks to the inner heart and soul, gracing the reader with the gift of faith. In this way, the Word of God speaks to each human heart directly.

# 6
# THE PRIESTHOOD
# OF ALL BELIEVERS

As a way to rebel against the abuse and corruption they saw in religious authorities, many Protestant reformers insisted that all believers are priests. This means that all believers can intercede for one another in worship at the altar and before God in prayer. Christ alone is the High Priest whose death guaranteed salvation for all who seek it. He is the only divine mediator between humans and God and he should not be replaced by anyone else. Before Him, all believers stand as equals. In addition, since the Word of God speaks to each human heart in the grace of faith, there is no need for a church official to open the way to faith and, indeed, dependence on such human mediation may prove to be a

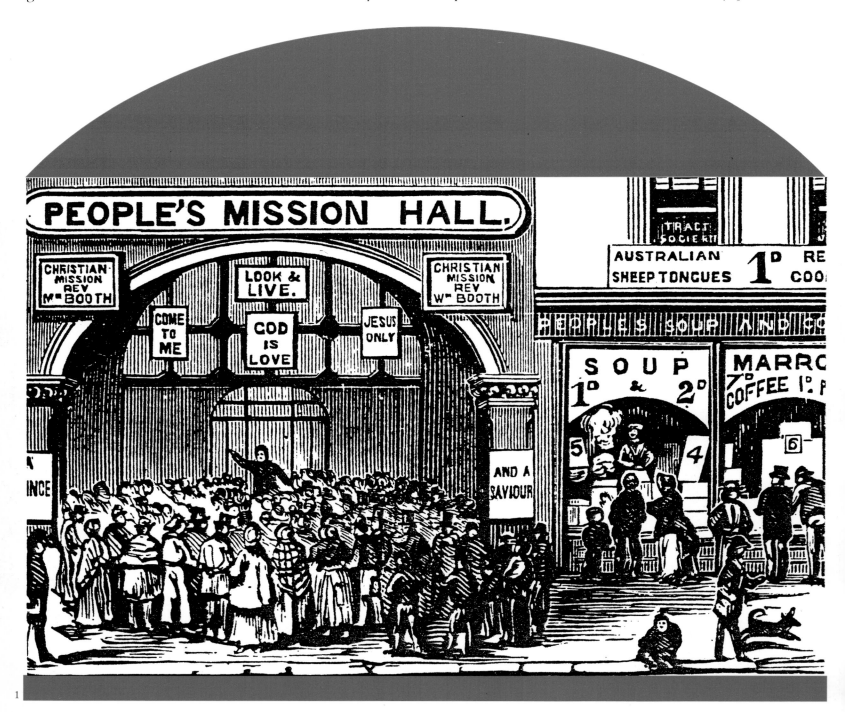

*1. A mission of the Salvation Army, founded in London at the end of the 19th century by the Methodist pastor William Booth, proclaimed the Gospel in the streets to those marginalized by society and also offered a bowl of soup and shelter, as shown in this engraving from the period.*

misleading obstacle. Since faith is a deeply personal experience of God as Savior and Lord, no one else can take your place—you must believe for yourself. The priesthood of all believers is a position that carries antiauthoritarian implications or at least an ambiguity concerning the theological value of a separate and marked authoritative leadership. In many Protestant views, when the conscience and intelligence of the reader are graced by God's Holy Spirit, which is a personal event, the reader guided by Scripture can exercise a right of private judgment that takes precedence over the determinations of the community and the mandates of authority. By decreasing the importance of the professional priests, the reformers also decreased the importance of the cult of sacrifice in the Christian community. Christ's sacrifice was offered once and for all. Instead of the daily Holy Sacrifice of the Mass as in the Roman Catholic tradition, the Protestant Eucharist, when celebrated at all, commemorates Jesus' Last Supper. Similarly, ordination to priesthood—recognized by Roman Catholics as one of seven sacraments instituted by Jesus—is not considered a sacrament in most Protestant groups. However, almost all Protestant groups have ministers, pastors, or professional clergy. The process of becoming a minister—ordination—formalizes the call to ministry from the congregation, in contrast to the Roman Catholic belief that priests' souls are impressed whith a special character. Finally, the priesthood of all believers allows many different kinds of people to be called to serve as pastors or ministers, including (depending on the denomination) not only men trained in a seminary who remain celibate for life, but a variety of men and women with different training and differing lifestyles.

*2. The drawing shows a female pastor focused on a religious celebration.*
*3. Here one sees an illustration of the announcement of the Good News that involves a whole family in a street of a typical North American city.*

2  3

# THE PROTESTANT PRINCIPLE

Protestantism is grounded in the abiding conviction that God alone is infinite and absolute; nothing in nature or history can be identified with God. Protestantism is dedicated to testify on behalf of God's unique sovereignty and to protest against any attempt to absolutize the finite, whether in the form of word, act, idea, person, institution, or any other cultural or material expression. This dedication is often called the Protestant Principle and it is tantamount to a constant vigilance against idolatry. God must not be equated with any one concept or any sensible reality. And since one should love God with one's whole heart and mind, one must also safeguard against undue attachment to anything that does not point beyond itself toward God. Whatever in this world makes a claim of unreserved allegiance must be denounced as idolatrous (perhaps even diabolical) and set back in proper perspective. In this sense, the Protestant Principle recognizes that it carries forward the protests lodged by the prophets of ancient Israel who denounced idolatry. The vigilance of the Protestant Principle ex-

tends not only to the outer world of history but also to the inner world of human creativity and imagination, raising doubts about the value of images born in the human imagination and concretized in human culture. All human realities must be held accountable to God's judgment or criticism. Whatever is human is imperfect; nothing within temporal human history or thought is beyond the cleansing criticism grounded in loving knowledge of the one, eternal God. The experience of God's goodness is a deeply personal event that occurs deep within the individual self, where the Word of God speaks to each soul. The surest path toward this conversation wherein the loving heart of God addresses and awakens in faith the loving heart of the believer, is the reading of the Bible, the inspired chronicle of God's grace. The Bible is God's living Word, kept alive by the Spirit who touches the grace-filled heart of the faithful reader. The Protestant Principle insures that nothing profane should ever usurp the place of the divine God in the human heart or anywhere else in time or space.

*1. A scene that reiterates how, according to the Old Testament, the Israelites met false prophets of idolatry. The followers of Baal, who were attempting to deceive the people, are seen here. Elijah dares them to invoke their divinity to send down from the heavens a fire on the place chosen for the sacrifice. Dances and rites take place, but there is no response from the sky.*
*2. Elijah, true prophet, invoking the one God, is able to show His power. In response to his prayers, a potent fire comes down promptly on his sacrificial altar.*

**3.** *The New Testament translated in French and published in Anvers in 1538. To the left Moses has his face covered after having received the Tablets of the Law; to the right, Christians who have received the Holy Spirit, have their faces uncovered, and on Veronica's veil, they can see Christ's face as shown to them by the Apostles.*
**4.** *Luther personally translated the Bible into German, vindicating the freedom of reading sacred texts without regard for official interpretations. Here we see the first page of his translation effort, published in 1523 in Wittenberg, where his reformation activities began.*
**5.** *The scene illustrated here shows a domestic prayer meeting in Reformation-era Germany, in which a family gathers to hear a Bible reading.*

# FAITH AND ORDER: DENOMINATIONS, POLITIES, AND THE STATE

A century after Martin Luther's death, hundreds of Protestant denominations already existed. By 1982, Christian sociologist David Barrett identified over 20,000 denominations in mainline Protestantism worldwide, as well as some 10,000 other organizational expressions of Protestantism. Many of the 225 denominations within the Church of England (also known as the Anglican communion or Anglicanism) would not call themselves Protestant, but instead would see themselves as the church Catholic as it has taken shape on English soil (as opposed to the Roman Catholic Church). Because the Church of England broke with Rome under king Henry VIII in 1534 and then carried out many significant reforms culminating with those in the Act of Supremacy enacted under queen Elizabeth I in 1559, other Anglicans do see themselves as part

*1. A meeting of the Calvinist congregation in Lyon (France) in the temple called 'Paradise' circa 1565.*
*2. Portrait of Henry VIII of England.*

*3. The ecumenical chapel of the Massachusetts Institute of Technology (MIT) in Cambridge, MA (USA) by architect Eero Saarinen. His sense of space and the light that infuses it from above express the inner relationship between the devotee and God.*

of the Protestant reform, and are viewed as such by Protestants, Roman Catholics and religious scholars.

The divisions among Protestants have sometimes stemmed from national aspirations, such as those in the Church of England or the state-established Lutheran church in Sweden, or from social identities, such as the African Methodist Episcopal churches, which are parent organizations of numerous African American independent churches formed at the beginning of the 19th century in response to racial inequality within North American Methodism. At other times, divisions among Protestants have come from different theological views of authority. Protestants have generally looked to the Bible and the early Christian community for their systems of government and decision-making. Protestants use several forms of government, including decision-making by bishops, by elected elders or presbyters, by synods or bodies presided over by elders, or by local congregations acting independently. These forms vary in practice. For example, the governing authority in some Anglican and Lutheran churches centers on bishops consecrated in an unbroken chain of episcopal consecrations descending from the apostles. However, when other Lutherans and Methodists consecrate bishops to serve in positions of authority, they call forth individuals to serve for the greater good of the church without regard to this chain of apostolic succession. Overall,

Protestants have been flexible in their forms of government. Having questioned authority in the form of the Catholic church, Protestants have understandably wanted a more flexible system for forming groups and establishing rules.

Whether ruled by an episcopacy, presbytery, synod or congregation, Protestants have been forced to confront the question of the relationship between their own system of decision-making and the authority of the local and state governments. Early reform movements, such as those begun by Luther, Calvin and Zwingli, generally followed the state-establishment model set by the Holy Roman Empire, though on a much smaller scale. In England, Germany, Holland, Scandinavia, Scotland and Switzerland, kings, legislatures and other ruling powers established Protestant churches and then gave privileges of the state to them. As time passed, many Protestants favored the separation of church and state, particularly in light of the experience of later forms of Protestantism which, lacking the favor of the state, suffered repression even at the hands of Protestant states.

Today, many Protestant polities, or governing bodies, belong to the World Council of Churches, founded in 1948.

*4. The General Assembly of the World Council of Churches in Canberra (Australia) in 1991.*

# RADICAL REFORM SECTS:
# PIETY, APOCALYPSE, AND MYSTICAL EXPERIENCES

Embodying the Protestant Principle, many Protestant sects have arisen to criticize the corruptions within church and society. Sects remain small, self-governing congregations, in deliberate contrast to larger churches that these sects view as too worldly. While church membership is usually the result of history or geography (being born, for instance, in a Lutheran family or state), sects ask for a special act of will on the part of new members. This usually involves a second baptism—baptism as a conscious act requested by an adult, rather than the baptism performed on infants. Such sects were called Anabaptists, meaning "rebaptizers." Anabaptists conducted an even more Radical Reform, using Scripture as the source not only of their faith, but also of their decisions, forms of community, and daily habits. Anabaptists were persecuted by Catholics and Protestants alike. In 1534-1535, Melchior Hofman, Jan Beukelssen (a tailor) and Jan Matthys (a baker) es-

*1. An image of the feast of Pentecost in an Armenian miniature from a collection of hymns of 1591.*
*2. In 18th century America, a Quaker meeting. Already well known in their native England for their intellectual independence, they founded a colony in Pennsylvania; they were always distinguished for their dedication to great social issues.*

tablished a community in Münster, Germany, based on the biblical principles of polygamy and shared property. Their effort was crushed by a combined Catholic and Lutheran military action. Following this defeat, leaders like Menno Simons, a former Roman Catholic priest whose followers are known as Mennonites, directed their sects toward pacifist beliefs, not supporting any military action on the part of their government. Puritan and Separatist sects in England criticized the established Church of England and favored separation of religion from the control of government. The first Baptist church returned to England in 1612 under the leadership of John Smyth after years of exile in Holland. Baptists received severe treatment in England through the 17th century. Under the leadership of William Brewster and William Bradford, Separatists from Scrooby in England moved to Leiden, Holland in 1609 and then to Plymouth Colony in America in 1620.

There are many sects in this Radical Reform movement of Protestantism, and they are quite different from each other. They include the Quakers, or Society of Friends, started by the English mystic George Fox (1624-1681), who stressed the value of sitting in silence during meetings. Later, Mother Ann Lee led a movement of Shaking Quakers, or "Shakers," from England to the United States, where men and women lived together in celibate communities that emphasized song and exuberant dance in worship. In Germany, Philip Spener (1635-1705) and Hermann Francke (1663-1727) formed small sects, known as Pietists, based on the quality of individual emotional experiences felt in response to Bible reading and prayer. The Moravian Brethren, who were founded in Germany in 1727 by Count Zinzendorf and emigrated to the American colonies soon after, owed much to Pietist influences and, in turn, influenced John Wesley, who began the Methodist movement in England and America.

Although some sects formed for theological reasons (such as Unitarians, who do not agree with the belief in the Trinity), most sects are based on three fundamental beliefs drawn from the New Testament: piety (the individual's strong emotional response to an awareness of faith and salvation); an apocalyptic belief that the Kingdom of God will arrive soon; and mystical experiences of extraordinary visions, signs and wonders.

Over the past centuries, Evangelical revivals sparked by sects have rippled through the Protestant world, inspiring new combinations of beliefs and styles of worship. From the 19th century mix of Radical Reform traditions (such as Baptists, Mennonites, Congregationalists and Quakers) with Methodists (who were influenced by Moravians), the Holiness Churches have emerged, and these, in turn, have become the launching pad for the Pentecostalism active around the world today. As the center of active Christian populations moves away from the Northern Hemisphere of Europe and America and toward the Southern Hemisphere of Africa, Asia and the Pacific region, the transformations of Protestant Christianity are likely to have a notable impact on the world's religious life in the third millennium.

3

**3.** *A dining room in a Shaker community, where men and women, seated at separate tables, took their meals in silence. After 1780, the Shakers created their own settlements to live in accordance with their own religious convictions. In Hancock, MA (USA) many Shaker buildings of simple and austere design survive the decline of their groups.*
**4.** *Lithograph from the 19th century that shows Shakers in a community dance.*

# "KNOWLEDGE OF GOD AND KNOWLEDGE OF SELF ARE CONNECTED"

*"Without knowledge of self there is no knowledge of God. Nearly all the wisdom we possess, that is to say, true and sound wisdom, consists of two parts: the knowledge of God and of ourselves. But, while joined by many bonds, which one precedes and brings forth the other is not easy to discern. In the first place, no one can look upon himself without immediately turning his thoughts to the contemplation of God, in whom he 'lives and moves' (Acts 17: 28). For, quite clearly, the mighty gifts with which we are endowed are hardly from ourselves; indeed, our very being is nothing but subsistence in the one God. Then, by these benefits shed like dew from heaven upon us, we are led as by rivulets to the spring itself. Indeed, our very poverty better discloses the infinitude of benefits reposing in God. The miserable ruin, into which the rebellion of the first man cast us, especially compels us to look upward. Thus, not only will we, in fasting and hungering, seek thence what we lack; but, in being aroused by fear, we shall learn humility [. . .] Thus, from the feeling of our own ignorance, vanity, poverty, infirmity, and—what is more—depravity and corruption, we recognize that the true light of wisdom, sound virtue, full abundance of every good, and purity of righteousness rest in the Lord alone. [. . .] Accordingly, the knowledge of ourselves not only arouses us to seek God, but also, as it were, leads us by the hand to find him. Without knowledge of God there is no knowledge of self. Again, it is certain that man never achieves a clear knowledge of himself unless he has first looked upon God's face, and then descends from contemplating him to scrutinize himself. For we always seem to ourselves righteous and upright and wise and holy— this pride is innate in all of us—unless by clear proofs we stand convinced of our own unrighteousness, foulness, folly, and impurity [. . .] Suppose we but once begin to raise our thought to God, and to ponder his nature, and how completely perfect are his righteousness, wisdom, and power—the straightedge to which we must be shaped. Then, what masquerading earlier as righteousness was pleasing in us will soon grow filthy in its consummate wickedness. What wore the face of power will prove itself the most miserable weakness. That is, what in us seems perfection itself corresponds ill to the purity of God."*

The quotation is the opening passage of
John Calvin's *Institutes of the Christian Religion* (1560)
Volume I, Book One, Chapter I.

(The English language excerpt is taken from Calvin: *Institutes of the Christian Religion.* The Library of Christian Classics vol. 20, edited by John T. McNeill and translated by Ford Lewis Battles. Philadelphia: The Westminster Press, 1960, pp. 35-38.)

**1.** *A man, alone and absorbed in his thoughts, walks in a present day Austrian town.*
**2.** *Albert Schweitzer photographed by Eugene Smith in Lambaréné, a village in Gabon, where he had founded a hospital and where he would live until the end of his life in 1965. Doctor, theologian and New Testament scholar, philosopher, and musician, destined to become a legendary figure, he well personifies the basic characteristics of the Protestant vision: mystic, that is sustained by mystery, and eager for moral responsibility, that is well disposed to active dedication in the service of others. Schweitzer was awarded the Nobel Peace Prize in 1952.*
**3.** *The exit of an Italian Waldensian church.*
*A woman embraces the sacred Scriptures: the spiritual enrichment of the ceremony, in fact, can only express itself in the personal engagement with the Word of God.*

# GLOSSARY

**Anabaptists** Members of the Radical Reform movement, who believed that baptism should be a mature testimony of faith, appropriate for adults rather than infants, and who wished to separate the church from the state.

**Apocalypse** The imminent destruction of the world.

**Commemorate** To remember an event or a person in a ceremony.

**Congregation** Christians who regularly gather together to worship.

**Contemplation** Devotional meditation on spiritual matters.

**Denomination** A group of religious congregations that share a common faith, name, and administration.

**Depravity** The human condition of moral corruption or sin.

**Disestablishment** The act of depriving a church of official government support.

**Dogma** A principle, belief or idea that is authoritatively set forth as true by a church.

**Episcopacy** A system of church government in which bishops are the chief officers.

**Eucharist** The commemoration of the Lord Jesus' Last Supper, when he ate bread and drank wine with his disciples before his death.

**Excommunicate** To exclude someone from membership in the Church.

**Grace** Divine love, sanctity, and power granted by God.

**Humanism** An intellectual movement dating to the Renaissance that emphasized the study of human culture, especially the liberal arts, and the study of the texts and arts that lie at the heart of classical cultures.

**Idolatry** The worship of false gods.

**Indulgence** Lifting the punishment due for a sin after it has been forgiven in the sacrament of confession.

**Inerrantism** Belief that what is written in the Bible contains no errors and is literally true.

**Infallibility** The capacity to state the truths of faith without error.

**Justification** To be made right with God; to be freed from the guilt and penalties attached to sin.

**Lectern** A stand that holds the Bible when it is read during religious services.

**Magisterial tradition** The official authoritative teaching of the church throughout history.

**Mass** Term used by Roman Catholics to refer to the sacramental commemoration of the Last Supper of the Lord Jesus.

**Mennonites** Members of an Anabaptist sect begun by Menno Simons.

**Methodists** Members of the evangelical Protestant church formed on the principles set out by John Wesley and his brother, Charles Wesley.

**Minister.** Person appointed to perform religious functions for the church.

**Moravians** Members of the Moravian Brethren, founded by Count Zinzendorf in Germany in 1722.

**Mystical** An experience of spiritual realities and divine powers not readily available to ordinary sensation.

**Omnipotence** The unlimited power and authority that belong to God alone.

**Pentecost** The seventh Sunday after Easter, when the Holy Spirit descended upon the disciples of Jesus in the form of tongues of fire.

**Polity** The form of government of a nation, church, or organization.

**Prelature** A church office or government run by a high-ranking member of the clergy.

**Presbytery** Government of a church by elders chosen to represent their congregations.

**Purgatory** A condition of the souls of those who have died in a state of grace in which they are purged of the effects of sins committed during their life.

**Quakers** Members of the Society of Friends led by George Fox.

**Redemption** Salvation from the sinfulness of the human condition.

**Synod** A church council or assembly.

# BIBLIOGRAPHY

BARRETT, DAVID B., ed., *World Christian Encyclopaedia: A Comparative Study of Churches and Religions in the Modern World, AD 1900 - 2000*, 2nd edition, New York: Oxford University Press, 1996.

FORELL, GEORGE, *The Protestant Faith*, Columbus, Ohio: Augsburg Fortress Publications, 1975.

HOLLENWEGER, W. J., *The Pentecostals: The Charismatic Movement in the Churches*, Minneapolis: Augsburg Publishing, 1972.

MARTY, MARTIN E., *Protestantism*, New York 1972.

NOLL, M. A., D. W. BEBBINGTON, and G. A. RAWLYK, eds., *Evangelicalism: Comparative Studies of Popular Protestantism in North America, the British Isles, and Beyond, 1700-1990*, New York: Oxford University Press, 1994.

PAUCK, WILHELM, *The Heritage of the Reformation*, rev. ed., New York: Oxford University Press, 1968.

WALLS, ANDREW, "Christianity," in JOHN R. HINNELLS, ed., *A New Handbook of Living Religions*, new edition, London: Penguin Books, 1997, p. 55-161.

WILLIAMS, G. H., *The Radical Reformation*, Philadelphia: Westminster, 1962.

# Index